Copyright © 2015 by Nick Nutter and Julie Evans
All rights reserved. This book or any portion there
may not be reproduced or used in any manner
whatsoever without the express written permission
the publisher except for the use of brief quotation
book review.

Editor Nick Nutter
www.visit-andalucia.com
info@visit-andalucia.com

Ebook design and compilation by
Julie Evans
www.wecandu.com

ISBN-13: 978-1519700803
ISBN-10: 1519700806

Contents

Introduction

The Story of One Bodega

Doña Blanca

Jerez de la Frontera

El Puerto de Santa Maria

Sanlúcar de Barrameda

Inside the Triangle

Exploring the Sherry Triangle

El Puerto de Santa Maria

Sanlúcar de Barrameda

A journey through time and space

Jerez de la Frontera

Introduction

The fortified wine known as sherry can only be produced within an area known as the 'Sherry Triangle'. The triangle is bound by the three towns of Jerez de la Frontera, Sanlúcar de Barrameda and El Puerto de Santa Maria, all in Cádiz province in Spain. A triangle formed by lines drawn between those towns encompasses an area of approximately 140 square kilometres.

The history of sherry is intimately entwined in the history of those

Sherry, an intrinsic part of life today   *Sherry from the barrel*

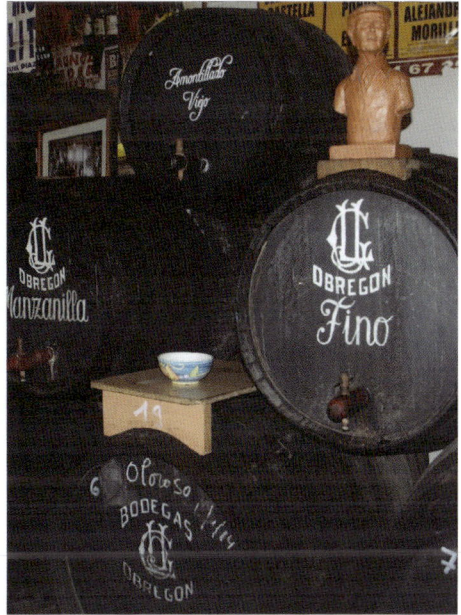

towns and the area between them. It is a history that can be traced back to 1100 BC.

The towns themselves are fascinating places in their own right, each with its own attractions and yet with a common denominator, the sherry industry. This book takes you through the history of sherry overlaid on the history of the towns. Today the sherry industry is not just a commercial venture, it has a prominent part to play within the tourist industry, drawing people from all over the world to the 'Sherry Triangle'. The amenities in the towns that form the triangle are as much a part of the story as the wine itself.

The Story of One Bodega

The González Byass company is one of the most famous and oldest established wine producers. Their maturation bodega is close to the cathedral in the centre of Jerez. The process of making sherry is common to all the large bodegas although the exact details of each part of the process is often a closely guarded secret kept by individual bodegas.

Many people think that sherry bodegas produce their wine from the grape to the bottled product. Some of the larger companies do but for many more this is not the case. The larger companies have a number of bodegas in the different towns of the 'Sherry Triangle' and perhaps a bodega or two in the grape growing areas in and surrounding the triangle. Each of those bodegas may have a different role to play in the production of the sherry. González Byass is an example of one company with many bodegas.

The Beginning

The González business was established in 1835 in Jerez by Manuel María González Angel. Manuel had an uncle Joseph who lived in Sanlúcar de Barrameda who enjoyed dry wines. Consequently when Uncle Joseph came to visit his nephew he brought with him casks of his favourite tipple.

Tio Pepe at Jerez de la Frontera

Tio Pepe

He taught Manuel how to turn the very dry wine into a pale, dry, fortified wine that became known as 'Uncle Joseph's' wine, 'Tio Pepe'. Manuel was the only native born wine producer in Jerez. The market was already dominated by the British who had label names recognisable today such as Osborne, Gordon and Terry. The first Tio Pepe was exported to the UK in 1844 where it impressed a wine merchant, Robert Blake Byass. He arrived in Jerez convinced that Tio Pepe had a great future and the González Byass partnership was born.

Whether the 'Tio Pepe' tale is accurate or not, it was in the early 19th Century that the producers of the sherry wine started to experiment with fortification, a practice the Portuguese had started to produce port wine. The sherry producers found that fortifying the wine after fermentation killed the flor, the yeast crust that develops on the wine, and allowed more oxidation that in turn produced a different wine, one they called oloroso, meaning 'pungent'.

A Walled Town

As the González Byass business expanded during the 19th and 20th centuries the premises were expanded, not by constructing new buildings, but by purchasing whole streets in the old town. The bodega is in effect a walled town of its own within the town of Jerez. Each street is carefully maintained and decorated with barrels of bright red geraniums. Between the roofs stretch wires along which grow vines, more for practicality, they shade the street from the roasting sun during the summer, than for the grapes they produce.

WINE FACT
González Byass started shipping sherry in bottles as early as 1839. Until then sherry was always transported in casks. At first any style of bottle was used for the sherry but by the 1870s a style unique to sherry was being used, the Jerezana bottle. This bottle becomes narrower towards the bottom and has a bulge in the neck and is made of dark glass. The style is still used for bottling special sherries.

Harvesting

The Palomino grapes are harvested in early September. They are first pressed lightly to extract the must, the primera yema. This is used to produce Fino and Manzanilla sherry. Must from the second pressing, the segunda yema, will be used for Oloroso. Any must from further pressings is used to make inferior wines and vinegars.

For naturally sweet wines, two other grape varieties are used: Pedro Ximénez and Moscatel. These are left outside in the Andalusian sun for between several hours and several days until the grapes lose some of their moisture and have a higher relative sweetness. The grapes will resemble raisins when they are crushed. Higher pressure is needed to extract the juice.

WINE FACT
A bodega is defined as a cellar or shop selling wine. In the Sherry Triangle a bodega can be any building involved with the growing, pressing, fermentation, fortification, ageing, warehousing or selling of wine.

Fermentation

After filtering the musts, correcting the pH and treating with sulphur dioxide to prevent bacterial contamination, the grape juices will start to ferment naturally. In days gone by this was done in wooden barrels (Valdespino Fino Inocente is still made that way) but nowadays most bodegas use huge stainless steel tanks that are heated to 23-25°C. Usually a small amount of already fermenting must (pie de cuba) will be added to speed up the initial process. After that, two phases

of fermentation (tumultuous and slow fermentation) take place. Musts of Palomino grapes will keep fermenting until nearly all of the available sugars are processed into alcohol – this will lead to a dry "base wine" ready around the end of Autumn. On the other hand the fermentation of the Pedro Ximénez and Moscatel musts will be stopped early in the process by bringing it to 10% alcohol, in order to retain a lot of the sugars. These wines are left to settle during the winter months and are then fortified to their final strength.

Old sherry barrel with glassfront and sherry content with a layer of Flor

At the end of the fermentation process, a layer of yeast cells, up to 2 cms thick, the flor, will naturally occur on these base wines, due to the specific climatic conditions of the Jerez area. The sherry obtains its unique flavour because of the 'sherry flor' phenomenon. Unlike other wines that have to be separated from the atmosphere during aging, sherry benefits from having an air gap between the surface of the sherry in the barrel and the top of the barrel itself. The aging wine is protected from the wine fly, which turns a normal wine to vinegar, by this ivory coloured, waxy foam. Since only one third of the wine is piped off at any one time the flor is repeatedly fed and thereby kept alive from year to year. Great care is taken when sampling and transferring the wine that the flor is not broken up. Flor, or the lack of it, produces two categories of sherry, biologically aged sherry that matures under the flor such as Fino and Manzanilla and oxidative sherry that matures only partially or not at all under the flor such as Amontillado, Oloroso or Pedro Ximénez.

Chalk strokes indicate the quality of the sherry in the barrel

Assessing the Wine

The wine is sampled at this stage to assess its potential. A single chalk stroke, /, on the barrel indicates a wine with the finest aroma and flavour. This wine can expect to be fortified to 15% alcohol to allow the growth of the flor by adding neutral grape spirit produced in the La Mancha region of Spain from Airen grapes.

A single stroke and a dot, /., indicates a heavier more full bodied wine that will be fortified to 17.5% alcohol to prevent the growth of the flor and the wine will be aged by exposing it to air to produce Oloroso sherry. A double stroke, //, indicates wine that needs to mature a short time and then be re-assessed, these wines are fortified to 15%. A triple stroke, ///, wine will be distilled. Naturally sweet wines will always be fortified to a higher degree as flor is not wanted in this type of sherry.

Maturation

After fortification the wine is transferred to a 600 litre oak cask. These casks will undergo a short period of maturation after which they are classified again and enter the solera system according to this final categorisation. Biological aging will result in a Fino or Manzanilla (if the bodega is in Sanlúcar de Barrameda) while oxidation will result in an Oloroso. The wines must mature for at least two years (a recent regulation, the minimum aging period used to be three years) to develop each style's unique characteristics.

WINE FACT
To qualify as sherry the wine must mature within the Sherry Triangle although the grapes themselves can be grown elsewhere.

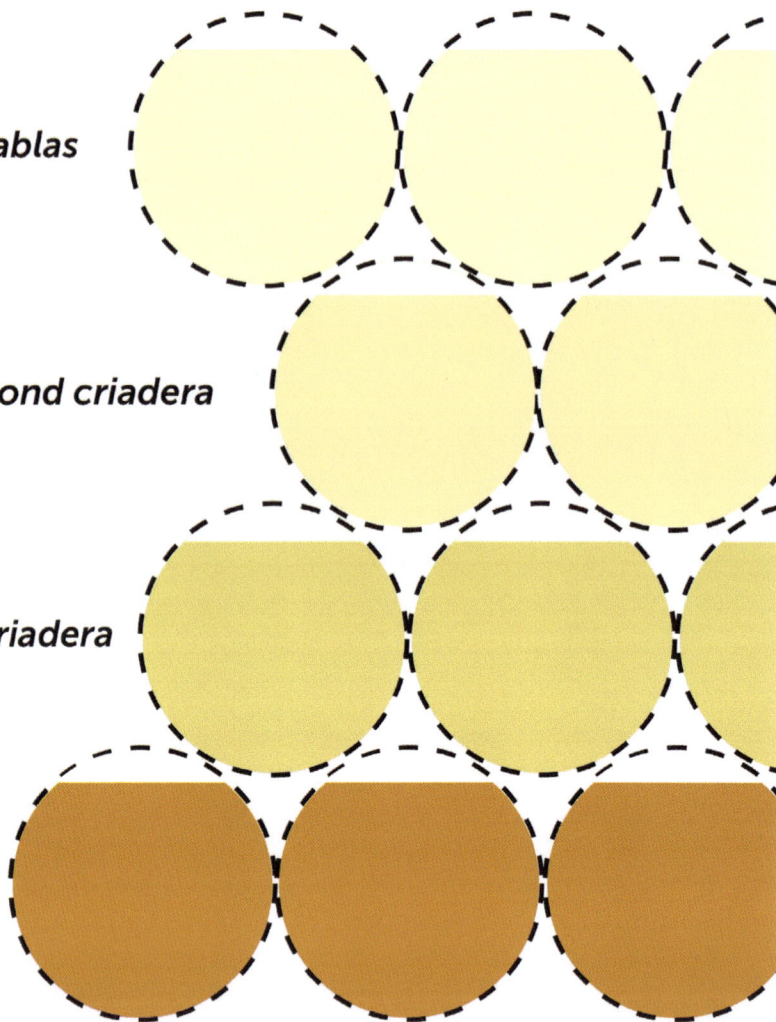

sobretablas

second criadera

first criadera

solera

The Solera

A solera traditionally consists of a number of rows of barrels called criaderas. Each row contains wine of the same age. The oldest wine, ready to be bottled, is on the bottom row (confusingly also called a solera), the youngest on the top row. When wine is removed from the bottom row or solera it is replaced by wine from the first criadera which in turn is replaced by wine from the second criadera and so on until you reach the top criadera which is topped up with new wine called sobretabla. This process may occur two to four times per year if the wine is a Fino and six to ten times per year if it is Manzanilla due to the higher activity of the sherry flor.

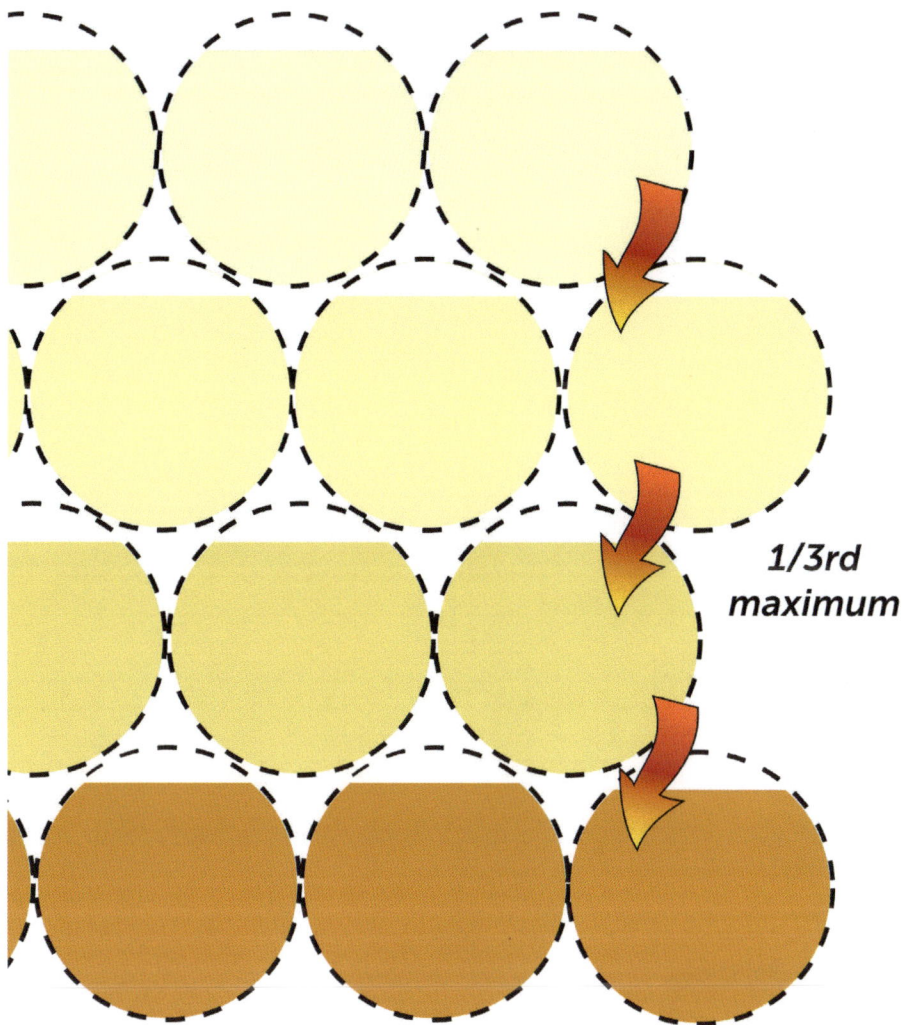

1/3rd maximum

Between 10% and 15% of the barrel will be taken out at any one time. The limit by law is 35%.

In a large bodega, unseen by visitors, the criaderas will be in blocks of casks rather than rows. Sometimes a whole room will contain just one criadera and one solera may occupy several buildings. The reasons for this are twofold. Since the system was devised back in the 18th Century it was found that it was better to have Fino and Manzanilla types close to the floor where it is cooler and the other, oxidative types of sherry towards the top. Secondly it was a matter of stability. More than three rows of barrels and the solera may collapse. There is more than one way to get a headache with sherry.

Classifying the Sherry

A typical Fino solera will have between three and seven criaderas whilst a Manzanilla solera may have nine to twenty. After a wine has been through the solera system it is impossible to give it an age. An approximate, average age can be determined and the average age has to be three years before it can be sold. However, when bottled, the final analysis is performed by a group of tasters from the Consejo Regulador who will reject any wine if it is immature. They also award VOS and VORS labels to wines that fit the flavour profile. VOS stands for the latin 'Vinum Optimum Signatum', sometimes bastardised to 'Very Old Sherry', and VORS stands for 'Vinum Optimum Rare Signatum' or 'Very Old Rare Sherry'.

In the 1980s the bodegas tried to commercialise their older sherries by giving them confusing names on the label such as Muy Viejo or Very Old Sherry. Consumers found it difficult to know just what they were buying and impossible to compare like for like. In the year 2000 the Consejo Regulador ended this ambiguity by introducing strict rules with fixed age boundaries. 2001 was the first year that some wines were accredited VOS and VORS. To achieve VOS status the sherry has to be of an average age of 20 years and for VORS it has to be an average of 30 years old. The difficulty as we have already discovered is to ascertain the age of a sherry after it has been through the solera system.

The Consejo Regulador overcame this problem by laying down a specific process that has to be followed. First the wine is laboratory tested for age using the carbon 14 dating system. This does not produce very accurate results for any object or substance less than a hundred years old, the minimum and maximum age range established is often greater than the supposed age of the sherry.

The second test is called the total solera quota. The bodega has to maintain a stock of the wine being tested that equals 20 or 30 times the volume that will be bottled and labeled at the time of testing. This is to guarantee that the average age will not reduce in between the annual bottling. Finally a Tasting Committee that includes one person from the Consejo Regulador and five independent external experts taste the wine. They are provided with a reference sample from the last assessment.

Oxidative Maturation

During the maturation process the veil of flor can die and wines that started their life as a Manzanilla or Fino can gradually shift towards oxidative maturation. This can occur after a certain age (because the nutrients in the base wine that keep the flor alive have been consumed) or because the cellarmaster decides to fortify the wine again to deliberately kill the flor. This produces the intermediate types of sherry: Amontillado and Palo Cortado which are technically similar wines but with slightly different aromatic properties.

There are also naturally sweet sherries, Pedro Ximénez and Moscatel. However some sherry is sweetened after maturation by adding a kind of raisin syrup or by blending a dry wine with a naturally sweet sherry. These produce the sherries that are labeled Pale Cream, Medium, Cream and Dulce. These wines may be put back into barrels to 'marry' the different components and then bottled after another period of maturation.

After the maturation the wine to be bottled will be in the final stage of the solera. It will then be filtered and stabilised. If necessary the wine will be fortified again in order to reach a certain alcoholic content depending on the type of sherry. It will also be blended, the output of different casks will be mixed together, and finally bottled and labelled. The González Byass house mature the sherry at their Jerez bodega and transport it to their El Puerto de Santa Maria bodega for bottling. From there it is taken to Puerto Real where it is shipped all over the world.

The Antarctic Expidition

González Byass are proud of their sherry export record. The bodega has a collection of 120 sherry barrels, each one with a coat of arms representing the countries to which the wine is exported. One is particularly interesting. The 'coat of arms' consists of an outline of the Antarctic continent. It transpires that supplies taken on Scott's ill-fated 1911 expedition to the South Pole included bottles of Tio Pepe sherry. Since Antarctica is not a sovereign state and consequently has no flag the continental outline was used instead. In May 1989, seventy-eight years after the 'Terra Nova' expedition, Rear Admiral Manuel Catalan, attached to the new Spanish Antarctic base, signed one of the sherry barrels in honour of that expedition. This is just one of the hundreds of barrels signed by famous personalities over the years. Each signing is by invitation only and the list includes Churchill, Margaret Thatcher, Sofia Loren, Prince Philip, members of the Spanish noble families and, on the top row, Keith Floyd.

Jerez de Añada

Many wine and sherry guides maintain that a Jerez de Añada is a myth, that they do not exist. If you look carefully, they do exist although they are rare. Prior to the introduction of the solera system in the 18th century, sherry was bottled as a vintage, i.e. from a single year. Almost all bodegas keep a barrel or two of sherry to one side, not part of the solera system. Because it ages faster than a solera wine this single barrel wine can be used to bolster up a solera if needs be. Until recently bodegas did not market these separately matured wines but, since the 1990s bodegas such as González Byass, Lustau and Hidalgo have started to bottle just a little.

Jerez de Añada is produced from the fuller bodied musts and produces Oloroso, Amontillado and Palo Cortado wines or one of the sweeter types. Typically the alcoholic content will be 20 - 22%.

Out of a total production of 20,000 butts, González Byass hold back just 200 butts to make Jerez de Añada. Each bottle is a work of art, a replica of the 'Jerezana' style bottle used around 1850.

Every label is handwritten, is individually numbered and signed by the chairman of the company. Each bottle is supplied with a handwritten letter with information about the wine. The years and types to look out for are, Oloroso 1963 and 1966 both released to the market in 1994 and Oloroso 1964 released in 1995. 1967, 69, 70 and 79 vintages were all Palo Cortado. The 1994 vintage was released in 2014. Expect to pay 100 - 300 Euros per bottle depending on the year.

Example of an old still

Brandy

Some bodegas also distil their own brand brandies. The brand names of the González Byass brandies are Sobrano and Lepanto. The latter is named after the naval battle of Lepanto in 1571, the first major victory of the Christians against the Ottoman Empire when the 'Holy Alliance' fleet of ships from Spain, Venice, Genoa and the Papal States captured over 100 Ottoman galleys, releasing thousands of Christian slaves.

The base wine is traditionally distilled in copper pot stills called alquitaras that are heated by a fire made of holm oak. Nowadays more efficient column stills are used. Normally only one distillation is required but double distillation produces a smoother spirit. After one distillation the wine spirit will have 60 - 65% alcohol and is called holandas after the home country of brandy, Holland.

The wine spirit is aged using the same solera system as is used for the aging of sherry The aged brandy is drawn off from barrels on the bottom row. Only about one third of the contents of each barrel is taken in any one year. This is replaced by younger brandy from the second row that in turn is replaced by brandy from the third and top row. The top row barrels are replenished with newly distilled brandy.

The barrels used for the maturing of the spirit are all old sherry barrels that impart a distinctive colour and aroma to the brandy. The holandas wine spirit is colourless as it enters the solera. The spirit slowly matures into brandy as it typically passes through six criaderas gaining colour at each stage, until when finally bottled it is a pale chestnut colour.

WINE FACT

Sherry Brandy is a spirit distilled from wine and to be called Brandy de Jerez it must be produced within the Sherry Triangle. It began to be traded in decent quantities in the mid 19th Century. Nowadays the Palomino grape is considered too precious to distil into brandy so the Airen grape is brought in from La Mancha and Extremadura. Only González Byass produce Lepanto brandy from the Palomino grape. Once distilled the liquor is matured in sherry casks that have been made from new American oak and soaked in fermenting wine or sherry for a couple of months. The longer the brandy matures in the cask the more sherry flavours it will take on.

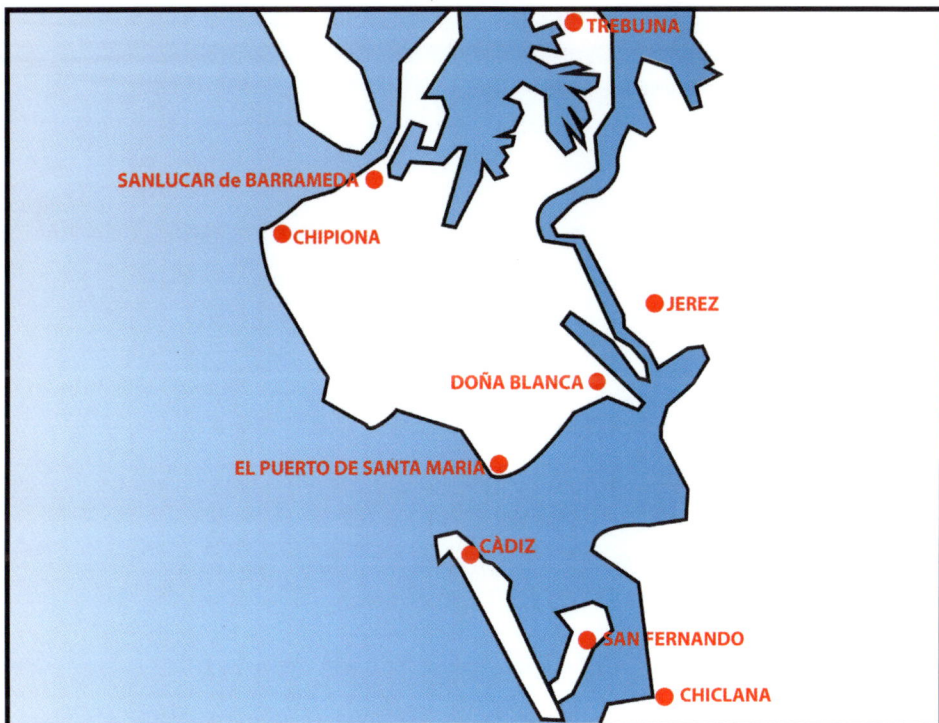

Doña Blanca

From Tartessians to Romans

Our history of sherry starts in about 1100 BC at an archaeological site called Doña Blanca, four kilometres east of El Puerto de Santa Maria and eight kilometres south west of Jerez de la Frontera.

In those days the Rio Guadalete that today flows in a narrow channel into the Bay of Cádiz at El Puerto de Santa Maria formed an estuary seven or eight kilometres wide from north to south and extending well inland as far as the location of Jerez de la Frontera, lapping the foot of the mound on which the settlement of Doña Blanca was built.

The Phoenicians meet the Tartessians

The Phoenicians, traders from the Lebanon area of the Middle East, had progressively, over a period of a thousand years or so, explored the north Mediterranean coasts looking specifically for

Looking down onto Doña Blanca and El Puerto de Santa Maria

metallic ores to supply the ever more voracious appetites of the Middle Eastern civilizations with whom they traded. About 1100 BC they arrived at a peninsula that would, after 850 BC, be the city of Gadir (Cádiz). In the estuary of the Rio Guadalete a few kilometres east, at Doña Blanca, they found the Tartessians already collecting and smelting the ores they sought and established a trading relationship with the inhabitants from about 750 BC.

The Tartessian civilisation's wealth came from the metal ores extracted from the ground in the hills in the vicinity of Rio Tinto in Huelva province and the range of hills that extend east and north east from there.

By the time the Phoenicians arrived Doña Blanca already had a long history. The first remains on the site date back to the end of the third millenium BC, the end of the Copper Age. It was later abandoned and re-occupied in the middle of the 8th Century BC.

A defensive wall was built around the settlement and a small harbour was built on the western side.

Tartessian ornamentation influenced by the Phoenicians

Ever the entrepreneurs the Phoenicians brought with them trading goods with which to purchase the ores, this was long before the concept of money, barter was the normal practice. Amongst the goods they brought from the Lebanon and the places they had traded with on their long journey to the Atlantic coast of Spain was a particular plant, the grape vine.

It was a fortuitous combination of factors, the vine itself and the area in which it arrived, for the low hills surrounding the estuary of the Guadalete are particularly good for growing grape vines as we shall see later in our history. The Tartessians planted the vines, harvested the grapes, and were shown by the Phoenicians how to tread them to extract the juice, the must. Already conversant with the process of fermentation of grains to make beer, the Tartessians needed little help fermenting the grape must to make wine. At Doña Blanca not only is there the evidence to show the Phoenicians traded with the Tartessians there, archaeologists excavated a building, probably of two stories, used for manufacturing wine. The first bodega, dating back to the 4th and 3rd Centuries BC.

Doña Blanca site of wine manufacturing c 800BC

Towards El Puerto de Santa Maria from Doña Blanca

The Greek Influence

As Phoenician influence declined their place was taken by
Carthaginian traders, (Phoenicians who in the 1st millenium BC had
established the city of Carthage that had then broken away from
the mainstream city-state political system of the other Phoenician
settlements) and Greeks who had been trying to break into the
lucrative markets of the western Mediterranean since the 7th
Century BC. The Greeks brought with them a dark sweet syrup
called arrope made from unfermented grape juice that was used to
sweeten dry wines.

Know your Sherry

FINO
The driest and palest of sherries ranging from bright straw yellow to pale gold in colour. It has a sharp, delicate bouquet with a hint of fresh herbs. Light, dry and delicate on the palate it leaves a fresh aftertaste of almonds.

MANZANILLA
Only manufactured around the port of Sanlucar de Barrameda. A bright pale straw coloured wine with a sharp, delicate bouquet with floral aromas. On the palate it is dry, fresh and delicate with a light and smooth finish. Manzanilla Pasada has been aged and partially oxidised giving it a nutty flavour

AMONTILLADO
Fino that has been exposed to the air producing a sherry that is darker than a Fino but still very dry. This is an elegant wine ranging in colour from pale topaz to amber. It has a subtle bouquet reminiscent of hazelnut and aromatic herbs. It is light and smooth in the mouth with a long, complex aftertaste.

OLOROSO
Exposed to air for longer than an Amontillado producing a darker and richer wine. Alcohol levels vary between 18 and 20% and they are the most alcoholic sherries. A dry sherry. In colour Oloroso ranges from rich amber to deep mahogony and has a warm, rounded aromas of walnut and wood. It is full flavoured.

PALO CORTADO
Aged like Amontillado for three or four years at which stage the flor either dies or is killed by fortification or filtration. In taste and character it is similar to an Oloroso with the bouqet of an Amontillado. Chestnut to mahogany in colour it has a deep rounded palate.

PALE CREAM
Ranges in colour from yellow straw to pale gold. It has the sharp bouquet of a Fino with hints of hazelnut. It is light and fresh in the mouth with a delicate sweetness that is pleasant on the palate.

CREAM SHERRY
Made by blending Oloroso and Jerez Dulce. Its colour ranges from chestnut brown to dark mahogany with a dense syrupy appearance. A strong Oloroso bouquet combines with the sweetness of roasted nuts or caramel. It is full bodied and velvety in the mouth with well balanced sweetness.

MOSCATEL
Ranges from chestnut to intense mahogany in colour. It has the characteristic Moscatel notes, sweet and cloying, with the presence of floral aromas and citric notes.

JEREZ DULCE
Also known as Pedro Ximenez are sweet sherries made by fermenting Pedro Ximenez or Moscatel grapes or by blending sweet wines with the drier varieties, which produces a dark brown to black, intensely sweet wine. It is rich with sweet notes of dried fruits and aromas of honey, grape syrup, jam and candied fruit. finish.

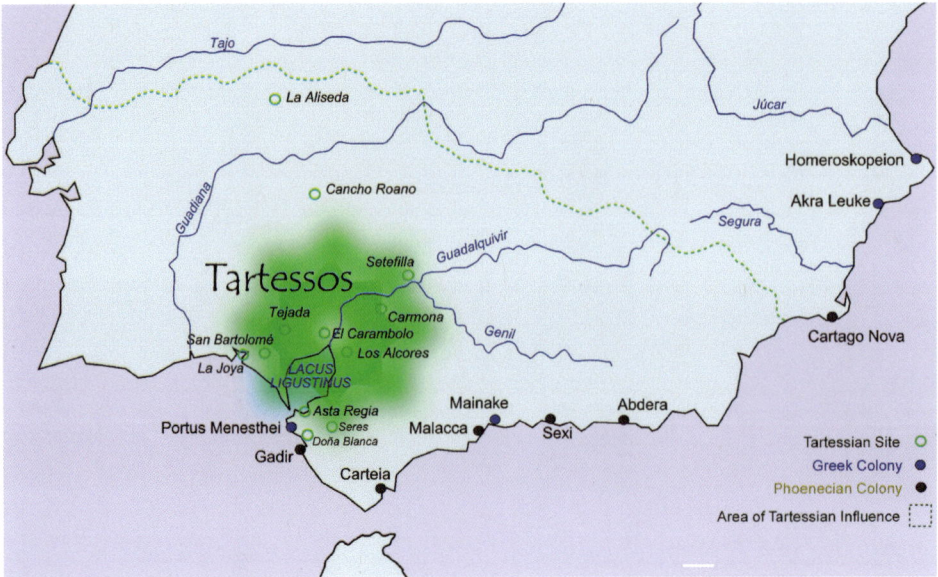

Map of the Iberian Peninsula showing Tartessos and surrounding settlements:

Tajo, Júcar, La Aliseda, Homeroskopeion, Cancho Roano, Akra Leuke, Guadiana, Segura, Setefilla, Guadalquivir, Tartessos, Tejada, Carmona, Genil, San Bartolomé, El Carambolo, Los Alcores, Cartago Nova, La Joya, LACUS LIGUSTINUS, Mainake, Abdera, Asta Regia, Seres, Portus Menesthei, Malacca, Sexi, Doña Blanca, Gadir, Carteia

Tartessian Site ○
Greek Colony ●
Phoenecian Colony ●
Area of Tartessian Influence ⬚

Jerez de la Frontera

What Is In A Name

As the trade between the Phoenicians and the Tartessians increased the Phoenicians established trading centres either within existing settlements or as purpose built settlements in their own right. A few kilometres around the coast (as it was then) from Doña Blanca, nestling in the mouth of the Rio Guadalete, was a Tartessian settlement. The Phoenicians called it Seres. The area was occupied by the Romans from about 138 BC and the name Seres was romanised to Ceret. There is no trace of a Roman presence in Jerez itself, they seemed to have confined themselves to another Tartessian settlement they called Asta Regia about 11 kilometres away in an area called the Mesas de Asta.

However the Romans, like the Greeks and Phoenicians before them, were not slow to realise the quality of the wine from this region. The wine became known as Ceretanum or 'wine from Ceret', possibly the first attempt to impose a classification on a wine based on where it originated, what we would now call a D.C. Ceretanum was exported all over the Roman Empire as far east as Constantinople and as far south as Libya. Amphorae with a

Roman Wine Amphora on display in Cádiz museum

stamp in the clay identifying the contents as Ceretanum, for tax purposes, have been found all over the territories occupied by the Romans.

The Visigoths and Vandals had a brief presence, they called the town Seritium, until the town was taken by the Arabs in 711 AD.

Once again the name of the town changed. This time to Seris, pronounced Sherish. The name was later to become the Spanish word Xerez and the English, Sherry.

> **WINE FACT**
> **The Greek geographer Strabo in the 1st Century BC in his book Geographica (volume III) writes that the first vines were brought to the Ceret area by the Phoenicians in 1100 BC.**

Non Drinking Islamics Take Over The Wine Trade

The first Arab occupiers of Xerez were non-drinking Islamics and they could have been a threat to the wine trade that was by now almost two thousand years old. However, they too realised that this wine was something special. After much debate it was decided that the passages within the Koran that forbade the drinking of alcohol should not apply to alcoholic beverages that were used for medicinal purposes. So that was alright then.

The second threat to the wine industry from the Islamic population came in 966 AD when Al Hakam II, the second Caliph of Cordoba, taking advice from his very strict Islamic vizier, Al-Mansur, ordered the destruction of the vineyards. The inhabitants persuaded him to spare two thirds of the vineyards on the grounds that the grape, dried, produced raisins that were used to feed the Caliph's troops. Another close call.

WINE FACT

It was the Arabs that introduced the process of distillation to the western world. Without distilled wine there would be no sherry or brandy

Wine Trade Expands Under Arabs

Despite being averse to drinking the product themselves it did not stop the Arabs expanding the wine trade to the whole of Europe. Henry I of England (1068 - 1135) negotiated a deal that exchanged English wool for wine from Seris. It was sometime during this period that the wine of the region was fortified with brandy distilled from the wine itself. Originally this was done to preserve it and make the wine more resilient to being disturbed as it was transported.

The 11th, 12th and 13th Centuries were a turbulent time for Seris. In the 11th Century Seris briefly became the seat of an independent taifa until, in 1040 it was united with Arcos and in 1053 it was annexed to Seville and became part of the emirate dependant on Grañada. The Almohads conquered the city in the mid 12th Century. In 1231 at the Battle of Jerez, Alvaro Perez de Castro, the grandson of Alfonso VII of Castile and Leon, defeated the Moors and the city was finally

Alfonso X of Castile

taken for the Christians by King Alfonso X in 1264. For the following couple of hundred years Jerez was situated on the border between the territories occupied by Christians and the Arabs, marking the edge of the Kingdom of Castile, and so earned the suffix, 'de la Frontera'.

Jerez de la Frontera Under The Christians

King Alfonso X himself established vineyards in the Jerez region and actively encouraged the expansion of the sherry trade. He also gave land to his military officers who had distinguished themselves including one Fernan Ibanez Palomino. Legend has it that it was this officer that introduced the white grape that later bore his name, the 'mother' of all Jerez vines, the Palomino that produces a white, very dry, smooth wine.

On the 12th August 1483 the growth in demand led the Jerez city authorities to make a proclamation of the Rules of the Guild of Raisin and Grape Harvesters of Jerez. These were the first rules of Jerez's Denomination of Origin and regulated the details concerning harvesting, the characteristics of the butts (known as botas), the ageing system and commercial procedures for the production of sherry.

All the ingredients and techniques required to make the sherry we know today were now in place. The right grape, the vineyards, the fermentation process, the distilling process, the aging and the fortification of the wine. Dozens, perhaps hundreds of growers in the region were producing their own fortified wines. Over the following centuries, as we shall discover, these processes were refined.

WINE FACT

In 1150 a cartographer called Al-Idrisi drew a map of the region. He clearly labelled the town of Jerez, Seris.

In 1967 the map was a key piece of evidence when the Jerez Sherry producers brought a lawsuit against the British Sherry producers for the improper use of the Sherry Denomination of Origin, proving that the word 'Sherry' used to denominate Sherry throughout the English speaking world is derived from the city of Jerez's former name.

The map is now kept in Oxford University's Bodleian Library.

Things to See and Do in Jerez de la Frontera

This is an opportune moment to leave the history of sherry and pick up that story in the next section. Meanwhile we will look at the other attractions Jerez has for the visitor.

Plaza Arenal

Perhaps a good place to start is the main square in the town, Plaza del Arenal. In the centre is a sculpture of General Miguel Primo de Rivera mounted on a horse. Rivera was born in Jerez and became dictator of Spain between 1923 and 1930.

General Miguel Primo de Rivera

The Alcázar

Just outside Plaza del Arenal and to the south is the Alcázar, one of the few examples of Almohade architecture in Spain. Remaining from that period are two gates, a small mosque, an octagonal tower, the baths, the Palace of Doña Blanca and the Villavicencia Palace.

As you enter the Alcázar through the city gate, the mosque is to your left. Whilst not being as large or elaborate as the mesquite in Cordoba it has a simple charm more fitting to its purpose. In the Villavicencia Palace, on the ground floor, is a relief model of Xerez as it was in the 12th century after the Alcázar was built. It is only when you see this model that you realize how extensive the city was at that time.

Arab water wheel next to bread oven

Evidence of old Alcázar

The Alcázar dates back to the 12th century although there is some evidence that it was built on top of an existing Alcázar dated to the Caliphate period of the 10th Century. It has had some more modern additions, the homage tower was built in the 15th century and the oil mill in the 18th. The most attractive part of the Alcázar has to be the gardens, laid out in typical symmetrical Arabic style, with an enormous sculpture of three horses and a number of small fountains. From the gardens there was access to the baths.

A Noria or Arab water wheel has been rebuilt next to the bread oven that produced food for the military establishment. The Noria supplied water to the oven and to irrigate the gardens.

Plaza del Cabello

Royal Andalusian School of Equestrian Art Foundation

You will find more horses in Plaza del Caballo, a giant sculpture of two bronze horses, and yet more in Plaza Mamelon. There you will see a monumental bronze of a carriage being drawn by five horses with an outrider. It is the work of Eduardo Soriano. It is no wonder that horses feature strongly for Jerez's second industry is training them. The Royal Andalusian School of Equestrian Art Foundation is based at Jerez.

Their famously choreographed performance, 'How the Andalucian Horses Dance' is famous throughout Spain. Visitors can see a show and tour the school that includes the training sessions, the stables, the Palace rooms, the Museum of Equestrian Arts and the Carriage Museum.

The Carriage Museum

Carriages drawn by onagers (wild asses broken to harness) were used in Ur in 2500 BC according to an illustration on the Ur

The Carriage Museum

Standard in the British Museum. Carriages are also called coaches after the Hungarian city of Kocs which became famous in the 16th Century for the innovative horse drawn kocsl (literally wagons), that were made there. Some of the first automobiles were also called coaches but, to distinguish them from the horse drawn versions, they were given the name 'horseless carriage' that later became truncated to cars while the horse drawn vehicles remained carriages. The power of vehicle engines is still measured in horse power.

The Carriage Museum has a fine collection of carriages from the 19th Century onwards including one used for royal weddings and some sporty little numbers driven fast by the rakes of the day.

Details of the times of shows, opening times of the museum and Palace and prices vary so check before your visit. The first week of May is the time of the Feria del Caballo when these beautifully groomed horses parade around the city and the school organises gala performances on Fridays and Saturdays.

French Carriage Clock

The Clock Museum

In nearby Calle Cervantes, if you have time, visit the clock museum.
On the hour, every hour, all the 302 clocks variously ring, chime,
ding and dong. On the quarter hour only the English clocks chime,
deep Westminster chimes predominate, and on the half hour it
is the turn of the French clocks, lighter tinkles and trings in the
background. The majority of the displays are unique pieces from
the 17th, 18th and 19th centuries, each spotlighted in beautiful
mahogany cases and each wound conscientiously every week by
the two employed clockmakers. The clock museum houses the
largest collection of working clocks from this period in the world.

English sundial clock with cannon

You will see the striking contrast between the French clocks and the English. The French were much more concerned with the decorative aspect of their clocks rather than the mechanism whilst the English clocks are less decorative but have more accurate timekeeping. The debate during the 16th century was whether or not a long pendulum produced more accurate time. Only later science in the 17th century proved that the length of the pendulum was important.

You will also see some unusual clocks including a portable English sundial clock. Portable sundials have been used for timekeeping since at least the 12th century. Later versions were aligned north/south using an integral compass. The gun clock also utilised a sundial. This was a more permanent structure. At noon the sun's rays were focused using a magnifying glass on the touchhole of a small cannon. This ignited the gunpowder and discharged the cannon, brilliant, unless it was raining that is.

The clock museum is open 10am to 3pm Tuesday to Sunday and at various times in the evening depending on the month.

The Municipal Archaeological Museum

The Municipal Archaeological Museum in Plaza del Mercado is worth a visit. This museum contains a 1st millennium BC Greek helmet that was dredged out of the Rio Guadalete close to Jerez de la Frontera. It is believed to be the oldest Greek object found in Spain. Other exhibits in this modern, recently refurbished museum, take you through the history of Jerez from prehistoric times to the modern day. Of particular interest are the cylindrical idols dating to the 3rd and 2nd Millenium BC, early evidence of a spiritual awareness.

Food and Drink

The population of Jerez enjoy their food and sitting out in an evening. There are any number of cafes and bars, most of which serve tapas. You will find many local dishes such as kidneys cooked in sherry, lamb cutlets in oregano and sherry and fish in a tomato and brandy sauce; you would be excused for thinking that water is a rare commodity in Jerez cuisine. Wherever you eat you are unlikely to be disappointed in the quality of the food imaginatively combined with the town's most famous product, sherry.

Jerez Marketplace

A visit to the thriving indoor market illustrates why. This is very obviously the place where the majority of people and restaurants buy their fresh meat, fish and vegetables. There is a huge fresh fish market with over fifty stalls selling fish from the auction at Puerto de Santa Maria, everything from giant tuna to boquerones and shellfish from huge spider crabs to diminutive Cádiz Bay shrimps, the latter piled in boxes and so fresh they are still leaping into the air trying to get back to the sea.

There is a similar sized vegetable market. It is packed every day with customers competing for the best buys. There is every seasonal vegetable imaginable, much of it from the nearby towns of Conil and Chiclana. The smaller meat market is an equal revelation with the usual beef, lamb and pork, enhanced with game in season, partridges, pheasants and rabbit from the campo.

The centre of the town is full of pedestrian streets with busy big name stores in between small bodegas where you can partake of the sherries and brandies from all the bodegas in town if you so wish. Shops observe the siesta so open in the evenings until 8pm or later. Restaurants and cafes open for dinner at any time after.

Ferias and Fiestas

Jerez de la Frontera is becoming famous for its ferias and festivals. In early May thousands of motorcyclists from all over the world congregate at Jerez for the MotoGP Grand Prix motorcycle racing event that is held at the Circuito de Jerez. This is one of the most watched races in Europe.

Just after the MotoGP, usually towards the end of May, is the Feria del Caballo, sometimes called the Feria de Jerez, one of the most important fairs in Cádiz province. This is celebrated in the Parque González Hontoria. It dates back to Mediaeval times when local farmers gathered to sell their animals, often horses. Bars and restaurants are erected in the park. They are called 'casitas'. In between admiring the animals or taking a turn on the fairground rides, you can wander in and out of the casetas sampling the food and drink.

During the last week of Lent, Jerez, as with many Andalucian towns, commemorates the Passion of Jesus Christ. The Catholic brotherhoods within the town perform penance processions through the streets.

The Festival de Jerez is a two week extravaganza of all things flamenco, dancing, live music, eating and drinking. Dates vary, the festival usually starts in mid February

Together with the national holidays and saints days there is hardly a week in the year that Jerez de la Frontera is not celebrating something.

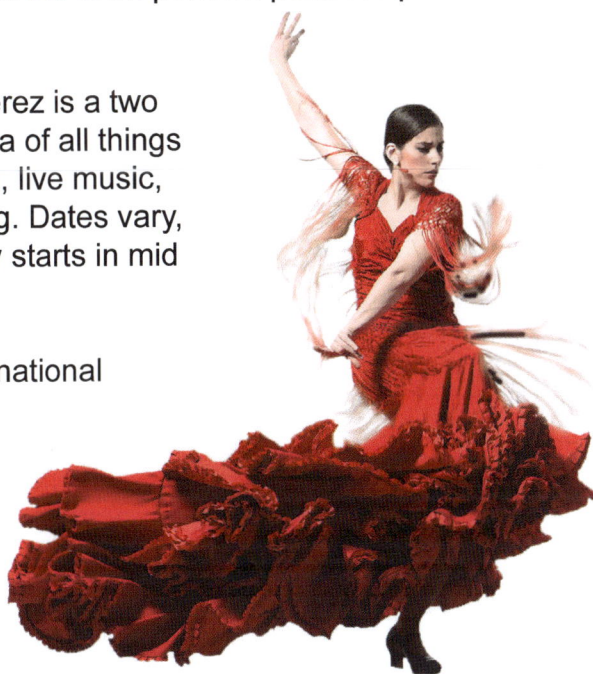

El Puerto de Santa Maria

The Town to 1492

We left the history of Sherry in 1483. It is now time to turn our attentions to the second point on the Sherry Triangle, El Puerto de Santa Maria. The port enters the story of the Sherry Triangle soon after the discovery of the New World in 1492.

The origin of the settlement that later became El Puerto de Santa Maria is shrouded in mystery. There is a local legend supposedly supported by Homer in his 'Odyssey', that after the Trojan War a Greek named Menestheus escaped with his troops through the Gibraltar Strait and established a town at the mouth of the Guadalete River. They called it Menestheus's port. If there is any truth to the legend the settlement they founded would have been established about 1275 BC. However it is quite possible that Homer was referring to the Tartessian settlement and port of Doña Blanca, that was at that time at the mouth of the river Guadalete just 4 kilometres east of where El Puerto de Santa Maria is today. Over hundreds of years the Guadalete estuary silted up and Doña Blanca became landlocked. El Puerto de Santa Maria is situated on

Looking towards El Puerto de Santa Maria from The Bay of Cádiz

the northern side of the Guadalette just upstream from its current estuary on the north eastern side of the Bay of Cádiz opposite and just 5 kilometres from that city.

Both the Phoenicians and later the Romans knew of the place which was renowned for its salt industry. The latter built fortifications on the site of the more recent castle which may well have established the town in which case it dates back no further than 138 BC. When the Moors arrived in 711 AD they named the town Alcante which means Port of Salt.

El Puerto de Santa Maria Under the Christians

The city was taken from the Moors in 1260 by Alfonso X of Castile. He renamed the town Santa Maria del Puerto and the town was granted a Royal Charter which allowed it to have the word 'El' placed in front of its name. Santa Maria del Puerto became El Puerto de Santa Maria. The town is in a strategic position. The Bay of Cádiz is a sheltered inlet some 5 kilometres deep, open to the Atlantic to the north west. Cádiz and El Puerto de Santa Maria occupy positions guarding the entrance. Both ports provided secure anchorage and berthing facilities and were important victualling stations.

The City of a Hundred Palaces

Following the discovery of the Americas in 1492 El Puerto de Santa Maria became the home town of a number of wealthy merchants who traded with the New World. They occupied grand houses of which a number not only survive today but are renovated and being used as hotels and government offices. The town earned the nickname of 'La cuidad de los 100 palacios', 'the city of 100 palaces'. It must have been quite a town. It was during this period that the fortunes of El Puerto de Santa Maria became entwined with those of sherry.

> **WINE FACT**
> **Following the marriage of Catherine of Aragon to King Henry VIII of England in 1509 she is recorded as complaining ' The King, my husband, keeps the very best wines from the Canaries and Jerez to himself'.**

Santa Maria reproduction at Palos de la Frontera

The town El Puerto de Santa Maria and the name of the ship The Santa Maria is a coincidence that has led to much confusion

New Markets in the New World

It was the discovery of the New World and the later voyages of discovery that opened up the next markets for sherry wine and it was the merchants of El Puerto de Santa Maria who saw the opportunities in this 'Immense New World' at the same time continuing to exploit the ever expanding markets in Europe. Wine was allowed to take up one third of the cargo space of ships venturing across the Atlantic and the merchants of El Puerto de Santa Maria took full advantage. El Puerto de Santa Maria became one of the two ports from which sherry was shipped, the other being Sanlúcar de Barrameda.

WINE FACT
Columbus took sherry with him on all his voyages to the New World. It was therefore the first wine to arrive in America

Sherry was taken to the New World

The English Thirst For Sherry

However the English thirst for sherry encouraged less scrupulous captains to capture the Spanish ships on their outward journey to the Americas and resell the purloined wine on the London markets. Sir Francis Drake went one step further in 1587 during the Anglo-Spanish War (1585-1604) when he sailed into Cádiz Bay and attacked Cádiz itself and made off with 2,900 barrels of sherry. The event became known as the 'singeing of the King of Spain's beard'. In fact for many years the wine was known as 'sac' or 'dry sac' but this may be coincidence since the Spanish word for extraction (from the solera) is saca. One bodega, Williams and Humbert, to this day still produce a sherry called Dry Sack.

Following Drake's return to London sherry became fashionable in the English Court. Elizabeth I herself recommended it to the Earl of Essex as the 'best of wines'.

William Shakespeare and his friend Ben Johnson used to drink a good few bottles of sherry every day at the Bear's Head Tavern. The Bard refers to it frequently in many of his plays; Richard II, Henry VI, A Midsummer Night's Dream, The Merry Wives of Windsor and Henry IV, amongst others. Shakespeare's character Falstaff was an ardent fan of the beverage (then known as sack), proclaiming: "If I had a thousand sons, the first humane principle I would teach them should be, to forswear thin potations and to addict themselves to sack".

With a rapidly increasing trend in the consumption of sherry, and faced with a scarce supply, James I of England decided to set an example by ordering that the Royal Cellars should only bring to his table 12 gallons (54 litres) of sherry per day.

The last attempt to steal rather than buy sherry occurred at the beginning of the second Anglo Spanish War (1625 - 1630) when Lord Wimbledon led a combined English/Dutch force consisting of over 100 ships and more than 15,000 men to Cádiz. The Cádiz Expedition as it was known, due to incompetent leadership, proved a farce and returned to the UK humiliated and sherry less.

The expedition did have one positive aspect. It persuaded English and Irish merchants that honest trade was the only way to guarantee their supply of sherry. The 17th and 18th Centuries saw the first of a growing number of wine merchants to arrive in Spain, some of the names will be familiar, Sandeman, Humbert, Fitz-Gerald, Gordon, O'Neal, Garvey, Mackenzie, Wisdom, Warter and Williams. Their arrival in Spain heralded the beginning of the Modern Age of Sherry.

WINE FACT
Almost since Drake arrived back from Cádiz with a surplus of barrels, Scottish whisky manufacturers have used the empty sherry casks in which the sherry was transported, for aging their whisky. The combination of the wood and the sherry impregnation gave the whisky a unique and individual flavour appreciated by connoisseurs. In the 1970s many bodegas started to bottle their wine before shipping it and the supply of empty barrels for aging whisky dried up. The whisky manufacturers turned to America and started to buy bourbon barrels. In the 1990s as this bourbon aged whisky started to hit the shelves the connoisseurs complained that the taste of their favourite tipple had changed.

The Modern Age

Up until the 'Modern Age' of sherry production, starting in the 18th Century, three types of business had been involved in the production of the sherry; vineyards, maturation bodegas, and bottlers and shippers (whose names appeared on the label). There were also a number of combinations. Some vineyards grew and pressed the grapes and then fermented and matured the must before selling it to the bottling and labelling business and some businesses concentrated on buying in the young wine and maturing it and then selling it to the bottling and labelling business.

The Almacenistas

Once the UK entrepreneurs arrived in Spain there began a general trend towards combining the vineyards, maturation bodegas, and bottlers and shippers in the name of efficiency. Today you will find companies such as González Byass that do produce sherry from grape to bottle in bodegas in Jerez de la Frontera and El Puerto de Santa Maria. Rarely will you find the other extremes, the bodega that grows the grape, produces the must and ferments the wine - most are large cooperatives, and the bodega that concentrates solely on maturation, the almacenistas.

Here in Puerto de Santa Maria you can taste a little of the history by visiting one of the very few maturation bodegas that are allowed to sell their own product. It is quite an experience visiting an Almacenista, it is like taking a quick trip back to the 18th Century.

The almacenistas buy young wines and mature them in soleras for several years. They are then sold on to larger houses where they are blended into the commercial product or incorporated into larger soleras for further maturation. The D.O. Jerez-Xérès-Sherry decides which almacenistas can export his wines or sell them to the consumer. Some almacenistas also ran a tabanco from which they sold their own products. One such tabanco still exists in El Puerto de Santa Maria, Tabanco Obregón attached to Bodega Obregón in Calle Zarza.

Here you can, if you wish, save yourself 60 cents and take your own litre container to have it filled with sherry from one of the casks, or you could just have a glass.

A combination of a decline in sherry sales worldwide and the trend for the cooperative grape producers to produce the base wine that they sell to the bodegas has meant a drop in the number of almacenistas, to less than 20. The Consejo Regulador tried to overcome this problem by lowering the minimum amount of stock for getting a shipping license, from 12,500 hectolitres to 500. As a result some of the smaller almacenistas can now bottle, label and sell their own product. Notable labels to look out for are, 'Bodegas Tradicion', 'El Maestro Sierra' and 'Fernando de Castilla'.

We shall pick up the history of sherry when we look at the town of Sanlúcar de Barameda. Meanwhile El Puerto de Santa Maria has more to offer.

WINE FACT
In 1830 Josés Antonio Sierra, a top cooper with González Byass, started his own bodega and became an almacenista. Old labels still show a hunting scene, nobles on horseback, hunting the 'little rabbit', El Maestro Sierra'. The best wines in the house are still preserved in casks made by Sierra himself.

Things to See and Do in El Puerto de Santa Maria

A tour of the town will give the visitor a better understanding of the sherry trade. Until the rail line from Jerez de la Frontera to Cádiz was built all the sherry from Jerez was stored in warehouses at El Puerto de Santa Maria before being shipped all over the world. Famous names like Osborne and Terry are written in large letters on the massive bodegas that occupy whole blocks near the port area. Many of these bodegas were established at the beginning of 'The Modern Age for Sherry'.

Fishing Industry and Romerijo

El Puerto de Santa Maria's second industry is fishing. The local boats bring in wonderful fresh fish from the Atlantic every day. After sampling the sherry there can be nothing better than a visit to Romerijo for lunch. This al fresco restaurant on the promenade specialises in shell fish and to obtain best value you have to do as

Seafood on display at Romerijo

the locals do. First go into the 'shop'. There you will encounter a huge range of precooked on the premises shellfish, some familiar, some not. Be adventurous, it's fun. Everything, from the smallest Cádiz Bay shrimp (an essential ingredient in crispy camerones or shrimp pancakes) to huge Norwegian lobsters is clearly marked for sale by the quarter, half and full kilo. Make your selection and pay. It will be wrapped in a paper cone. Take your fish to a vacant table. In the summer and at weekends be warned, after 2pm there is little chance of a table immediately. A waiter will offer you a menu so you can chose salads, bread and wine to go with your fish. Fino sherry is an excellent accompaniment. He will also bring your plates, cutlery, skewers for prising the meat out of shells and claw crackers. That's it, enjoy. If you go back to the 'shop' for more make sure you leave somebody at the table or it will be occupied when you return.

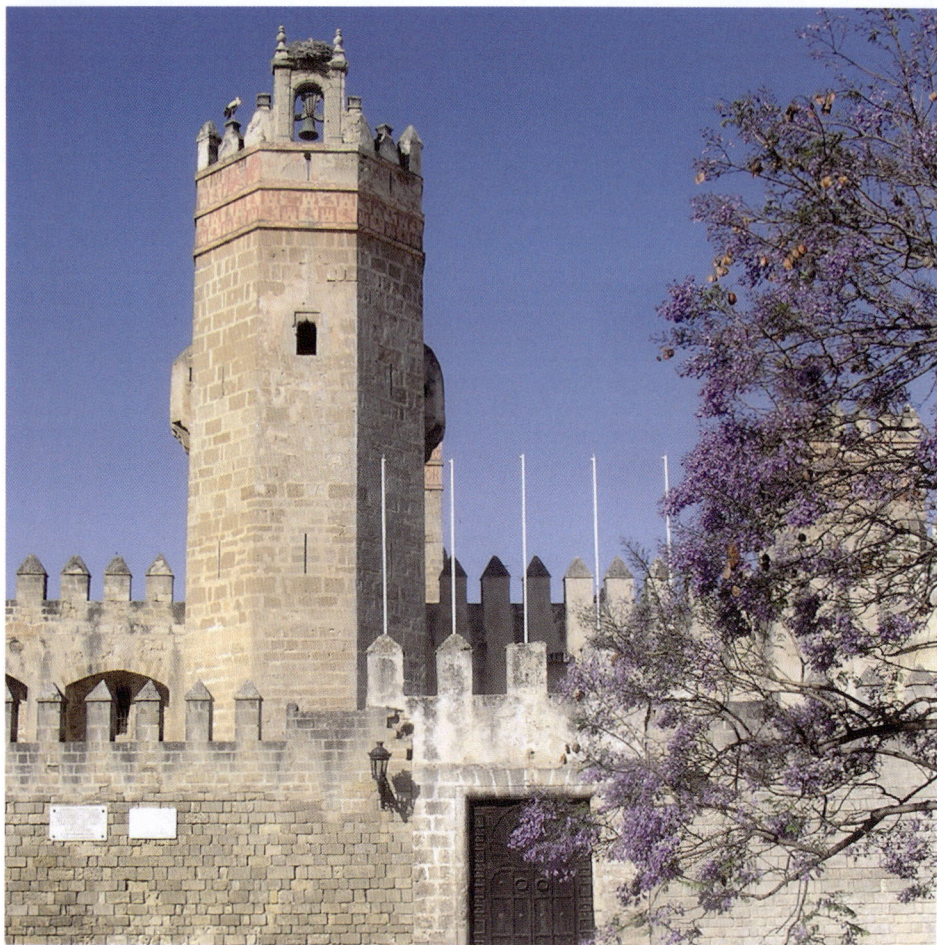

San Marcos Castle

Founded in the 13th Century on the site of a 10th Century mosque and the Roman fortifications, the San Marcos castle is now the geographical centre of the town. It was built to protect the then small village from pirates and it was here that, in 1492, Christopher Columbus tried unsuccessfully to persuade the resident Duke of Medinaceli to finance his first voyage of discovery across the Atlantic. It was in this castle that the trader, Juan De La Cosa, who supplied Columbus's three ships, the Santa Maria the Pinta and Niña, drew his world map in 1500 that first showed the American continent. Columbus never liked the ship the Santa Maria and he was relieved to transfer his command to the Nina when the Santa Maria foundered on rocks on the coast of Hispaniola on the first voyage.

Mastadon tusk on display in El Puerto de Santa Maria museum

Religious Edifices

The town also has a surprising number of religious edifices; four convents, two monasteries, four churches and chapels and one hermitage. The main church, appropriately called Iglesia Mayor Prioral was founded in 1486. Damaged in an earthquake in the 17th Century it was partly rebuilt in the Baroque style. The church now contains both Gothic and Baroque architecture.

Archaeological Museum

Opposite the Iglesia Mayor Prioral is the local museum. As you enter the first exhibit is a Mastadon tusk from a long extinct species that lived in Florida. It was presumably brought back by one of the merchants. Inside you will find artefacts from the archaeological site of Doña Blanca, once occupied by that almost mythical people the Tartessians and situated just east of the town.

Ferry Across the Bay

For centuries El Puerto de Santa Maria has been linked to the city of Cádiz by a ferry. First a rowing and sailing craft, then a succession of motorised vessels, the last of which was retired recently, and now by catamaran that can make the journey across the Bay of Cádiz in a fraction of the time taken to drive round.

Port Bonanza north east of Sanlúcar de Barrameda

Sanlúcar de Barrameda

The Age of Exploration

Sanlúcar de Barrameda, the third point on the 'Sherry Triangle', could be described as a modern old town, in this case not a contradiction in terms. The buildings date from the 15th Century right through to the 20th but somehow manage to sit side by side in a pleasing blend of architectural styles.

Situated at the mouth of the Rio Guadalquivir it was for a long time an important port (the actual port of Sanlúcar de Barrameda, is called Bonanza and is a couple of kilometres north east up the Rio Guadalquivir) and home to some famous explorers. Alonso Fernandez de Logo who conquered La Palma in the Canary Islands in 1492 and Tenerife in 1495 was born here. Columbus departed from Sanlúcar de Barrameda in 1498 on his third exploration of the New World and the Portuguese navigator, Ferdinand Magellan sailed from here in 1519, intending to sail around the world.

Unfortunately he never made it himself, being killed by natives in the Philippines but 'Nao Victoria' his last remaining ship of the five that started the journey, arrived back at Sanlúcar de Barrameda in 1522. Of the 237 crew members of all the ships only 18 returned home commanded by Juan Sebastian Elcano.

The Decline of Sanlúcar de Barrameda

Sadly, for Sanlúcar de Barrameda, events conspired to make the town a bit of a backwater. Until 1717 Seville hosted La Casa y Audiencia de Indias, otherwise known as the Casa de Contratación. This government agency tried to control the exploration and colonisation of the New World. The Casa collected all colonial taxes and duties, approved all voyages of exploration and trade, maintained secret information on trade routes and new discoveries, licensed captains, and administered commercial law. In theory, no Spaniard could sail anywhere without the approval of the Casa. Whilst the Casa was at Seville the town and port of Sanlúcar de Barrameda, at the mouth of the river that led to Seville, up which the treasure fleets sailed, was an important anchorage in a strategic position. Ships would also provision here for their outward journey. In 1717 the Casa removed to Cádiz and Sanlúcar de Barrameda lost its major source of income.

Fortunes changed a little in the early 19th Century as we enter the 'Modern Age of Sherry' and the economy of the town turned towards viticulture and tourism. We return to the history of sherry where we left it in El Puerto de Santa Maria in the late 18th Century. In the last years of the 18th Century Sanlúcar de Barrameda made two important contributions to the sherry industry, the solera system and Manzanilla sherry.

> **WINE FACT**
> *The vineyards in the Jerez region were an important source of wealth for the kingdom. In 1402, King Enrique III of Castile prohibited the uprooting of even a single vine by Royal Decree. He even went as far as to ban the placement of beehives in close proximity to the vineyards in case the bees damaged the grapes.*

The Extractors Action and the Solera System

The wines of the late 18th Century were not ones we would recognise today. They were young wines from that year's harvest, heavily fortified in order to preserve them during transportation. However the taste in wines, at least in Britain, was changing. Customers were wanting stronger wines with more colour and maturity. The rules of the Vintner's Guild, an organisation dominated by vine growers, however, prohibited the storing of wines of different vintages basically restricting sales to the current year wines only.

In 1775 the 'Extractors Action' lawsuit began, instigated by local producers and numerous foreign traders who had settled in the area. It took decades but eventually the Vintners Guild was abolished altogether. In the meantime the restrictive rules were relaxed and ignored. This left the way open for the introduction of the solera system of maturing sherry.

The Solera System is believed to have originated in Sanlúcar de Barrameda during this period in the second half of the 18th century. Prior to this, all sherries were bottled as Añadas or vintages, a concept that was still widely in use until the 20th century. Some of the oldest soleras still in use are now at Osborne (Capuchino laid down in 1790 and Sibarita in 1792), El Maestro Sierra (1830), Valdespino (1842) and González Byass (1847).

The combination of the solera system, the flor and the fortification of the wine, at first a method of making it more robust but now an integral part of producing a new wine, gradually turned the art of making sherry into a science.

Manzanilla Sherry

WINE FACT
Tabancos, peculiarly Andalucian establishments, started opening in the 17th Century. They were half tavern, where you could have a drink and something to eat, and half wine shop. Nowadays a tabanco serves all kinds of sherry direct from the barrel. Often the place will not have tables and chairs or stools, just upturned barrels on which to place your glass and plate. The name comes from a combination of estanco, - state run shops that sell stamps and alcohol, and tobacos - cigarette shops.

The wine makers of Sanlúcar noticed that barrels of wine left to age in bodegas open to the sea air developed a lighter, crisper, more apple like flavour than other sherries. They also noticed that the flor was more active and less robust. Barbadillo bottled its first Manzanilla in 1821 but it was not until 1964 that the specific appellation Manzanilla - Sanlúcar de Barrameda was created.

Only sherry wines matured in Sanlúcar de Barrameda can carry the word Manzanilla on the label.

Manzanilla Pasada has been aged and partially oxidised giving it a nutty flavour.

Things to See and Do in Sanlúcar de Barrameda

It is only by walking through this town that you obtain a hint of its involvement with the sherry trade. Standing in the two main squares, one with a straight, wide, boulevard that leads to the estuary, all the buildings on one side date from the 16th and 17th Centuries whilst all those on the other are 18th to 20th. As you head deeper and up into the town the buildings become older until you reach the oldest part, the 15th Century Castillo de Santiago opposite which is the Barbadillo Bodega. On the way you will have passed the Palacio de los Duques de Orleans y Borbon, now the town hall, and the Palacio El Ducal de Medina Sidonia.

Just above the Municipal Market is the so called sea gate through the old town walls with a long, straight, steep, cobbled road leading directly to what used to be the quays. You will also have passed a number of bodegas where the Manzanilla sherry for which this town is famous, is stored prior to shipping it to all parts of the world. It is said that the west wind, from the sea, has a certain salty tang that lends a particular aroma and taste to the sherry and the bodegas that are in the path of that wind produce the best Manzanilla.

This may be true, when the west wind blows all you can smell in the streets is the heady aroma of fine sherry, quite intoxicating. Many of the bodegas are open to the public. The Gitana bodega shop in the main boulevard leading to the sea has a wonderful range of Manzanilla, Amontilado and Cream Sherries and brandies from the bottles you can pick up in supermarkets to rare vintages you will find nowhere else.

Castillo de Santiago

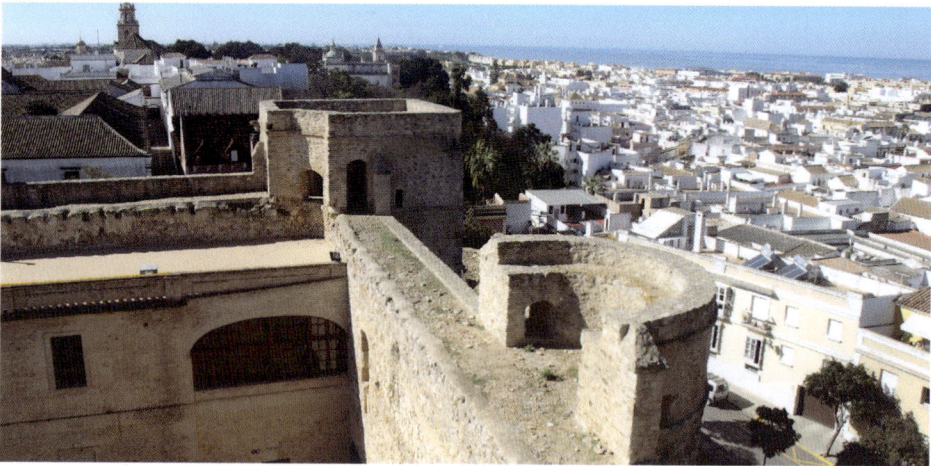
Sanlúcar de Barrameda from Castillo de Santiago

Castillo de Santiago

The Castillo de Santiago was built by Don Enrique Perez de Guzman, the 2nd Duke of Medina Sidonia, 7th Lord of Sanlúcar at the end of the 15th Century. At the time he was, except for the monarch, the most powerful man in Castile. In 1477, when the castle was completed, Queen Isabella of Castile looked out of a window in the keep tower and saw the sea for the first time. The modern day Keep houses an interesting exhibition of cartography that concentrates on the Atlantic coast and Cádiz Bay.

Doñana Museum

On the opposite bank of the Guadalquivir is the Doñana national park, a huge area of wetlands. Sanlúcar de Barrameda actually advertises itself as the Puerta de Doñana but if you expect to drive there from Sanlúcar de Barrameda forget it, it's all of 150

Looking towards Doñana from the ferry terminal

kilometres up to Seville and round to El Rocio, the main town in the Doñana. There is a passenger ferry across the river but then you are on foot or part of a four hour guided tour that whisks you around in a mini bus with little time to catch breath never mind study the flora and fauna. You can follow the signs to the Puerta de Doñana and, just before the grandly signposted ferry landing stage that turns out to be a beach, visit the Doñana museum which is in an abandoned ice factory.

The ground floor is devoted to the Doñana, its geography, geology, history and inhabitants, plant and animal and is very well done. The upper floor carries displays illustrating the history of Sanlúcar de Barrameda, concentrating on the explorers and overseas trade from the Phoenicians to the present day, and is similarly excellent, and free. It is better to visit the Doñana itself on another day.

> **WINE FACT**
> *Magellan purchased 417 wineskins and 253 kegs of Sherry before setting out on his voyage, spending more on sherry than weapons. Sherry, therefore, was the first wine to make a complete trip around the world assuming of course, there was any left by the time the Nao Victoria returned to Sanlúcar de Barrameda.*

Cádiz Bay Shrimps

Food and Drink

Eating in Sanlúcar de Barrameda is no hardship as long as you enjoy fish and anything else that comes from the sea; head for the area known as the Bajo de Guia. There you will be able to sample the delicious langostinos for which Sanlúcar de Barrameda is well known or the incredibly calorific camerones, small pancakes that contain handfuls of those tiny, exquisite, Cádiz Bay shrimps.

Self service tapas has reached new heights in Sanlúcar de Barrameda. Many establishments serving food, from bars to full restaurants, allow you to choose from a menu and from the spread of daily specials. You can specify tapa (snack), media racione (half portion) or a racione (full) portion. You wait for your choice to be cooked and then you take it to your table. Do not forget to ask for a Manzanilla. You will be served with an ice cold half bottle and as many glasses as you want. If you want more food or drink just go back. How they keep track of who owes what is a mystery but, after a couple of half bottles, who cares?

Stunning beaches for the horse racing

Ferias and Fairs

Samples of all the sherries produced in Sanlúcar de Barrameda can be tried at the annual Feria de Manzanilla that is held towards the end of May.

Sanlúcar de Barrameda is home to one of the oldest horse races in Europe and the first regulated horse races in Spain. The Carreras de Caballos take place just before sunset along the beach at the mouth of the river over distances of 1,500 and 1,800 metres. Every August thousands of people flock to the town to watch the spectacle. Only slightly less popular is the horse racing week for children and teenagers, again on the beach, starting on the bank holiday around the 6th or 8th December.

July, August and September are one long party on Saturdays; you will find flamenco singing and dancing competitions throughout the town. There is also an antiques fair and the International Classical Music Festival, 'A Orillas del Guadalqivir', on the banks of the river Guadalquivir. Every year Sanlúcar de Barrameda hosts a tapas fair, a local gastronomy competition towards the end of October.

Inside the Triangle

The Agricultural Triangle

Industry inside and surrounding the 'Sherry Triangle' consists of agriculture, growing vines of course as well as sunflowers and some cereals, sugar manufacture from sugar beet and solar farms. As land is cleared of vines, either because the crop is no longer financially viable or because the vines have reached the end of their productivity, it will be used for one of the alternatives. If the land is to be replanted with vines it will be allowed to rest for three years.

The low lying land gently undulates with plots delineated by raised tracks used by farm machinery and access roads to the fincas that dot the landscape.

Soil Types and Grapes

The D.O. Jerez-Xérès-Sherry does not allow any irrigation of the vines grown to produce the grapes used for the manufacture of sherry. That means the vines have to tolerate summer temperatures of over 40 degrees C with no more water than that which falls during the brief but heavy storms during the winter. On average the winter storms actually put down 620 litres of water per square metre. All of which would evaporate within a couple of months if it were not for the soils on which the vines are grown.

The soil considered the best for vines is called Albariza. In colour when dry it is white, composed of between 30% and 80% chalk and the rest is a mixture of limestone, clay and sand. It is capable

Acres of vineyards Inside the Triangle

of retaining huge quantities of water and as soon as the sun dries the surface a crust forms that prevents further evaporation. In autumn the earth may be 'banked up' which produces small reservoirs for water. In spring the soil is levelled

Albariza soil

off again. It is perfect for the Palomino grape vine. Pedro Ximénez grapes also like Albariza soil but few are now grown on it, it is cheaper to bring them in from the Montilla - Moriles area which is about 140 kilometres north east of Jerez de la Frontera, in the province of Cordoba, right in the centre of Andalucia.

The second choice is Barros soil. This is a rich dark brown soil, only 10% chalk with clay and organic matter. Barros is found at the foot of hills and in river valleys. More fertile but harder to work these soils produce more grapes than Albariza but they are of a lower quality. Grapes from Barros soil will not be used to make fino sherry.

Arenas soils are the least favoured. They are yellow, reddish soils with 10% chalk and a high sand content. They are found in the coastal areas of Chipiona, Rota and El Puerto de Santa Maria. Arenas does not hold water well and is only suitable for Moscatel grapes that will grow just about anywhere.

Pagos

Within the bounds of the 'Sherry Triangle' and on suitable ground outside the triangle the land on which vines are grown is divided into parcels called pagos. Although many of the pagos disappeared during the 1970's and 80's due to the reduced demand for sherry, about 60 still exist ranging in size from 2 acres to 1,500 acres. The finest pagos form a small area in the Jerez de la Frontera municipality called the 'Jerez Superior'. Every single pago has a unique fingerprint that can be detected in the finished wine, by those who know what they are looking for.

The oldest and best pago in the Jerez area is called Macharnudo. This area was planted with vines 3,000 years ago. Other notable pagos in the Jerez area are Carrascal and Añina. In Sanlúcar de Barrameda the finest pago is Miraflores whilst in El Puerto de Santa Maria look for sherries from the Balbaina and Los Tercios pagos.

The Carrascal pago is the furthest one inland and so is less influenced by the sea air. Grapes tend to ripen earlier and produce more robust wines, perfect for Oloroso. Macharnudo has a pure limestone soil and is at a high elevation. Its wines show a characteristic chalky quality. Balbaina, Los Tercios and Añina are near El Puerto de Santa Maria with exposure to the poniente winds. They produce lighter, elegant wines.

Even within individual pagos there may be vineyards in zones considered more favourable than others. Those vineyards became brand names in their own right. Some examples include Viña Botaina, Viña El Majuelo (the castle that adorns the labels of old Pedro Domecq bottles), Viña AB that is now labeled Amontillado Viña AB or Pastrana near Sanlúcar.

Working Pagos near Jerez de la Frontera

Historically sherry bodegas had their own vineyards and could aim for a particular character in the sherry they produced, sadly many sold out to cooperatives. Combined with the increase in mechanization, particularly for harvesting the grapes, the cooperatives have been responsible for a depopulating of the land. Dotted around the pagos are poignant reminders of those earlier days, fincas either abandoned or converted into holiday homes. Many display a sign at their drive entrance detailing the history of the building.

Cooperative growing also meant that individuality was lost and the expansion and industrialization of the 1960s demanded more volume and lower costs at the expense of quality. There are very few individual vineyard wines left. Two notable exceptions are Valdespino Inocente and Tio Pepe.

WINE FACT
New vines are planted and nurtured for three years before they produce a crop of grapes. In Jerez, each vine is commonly trained in the traditional manner of vara y pulgar, in which growers prune alternate spurs each year: one year's vara (stick) will be pruned back after harvest to become the following year's pulgar (thumb). Once established a vine can be productive for between 20 and 25 years.

19th Century Expansion of the Sherry Industry

During the 19th Century the sherry industry expanded enormously. Huge bodegas were built in the towns of the 'Sherry Triangle' and progress was being made into understanding and therefore controlling the complex processes that make a sherry. A narrow gauge railway ran through the streets of Jerez collecting barrels and taking them to the main line where they were taken to Cádiz. Sherry houses expanded, bought vineyards, amalgamated and diversified but then disaster struck.

Phylloxera

In the late 19th Century phylloxera devastated the vineyards. Phylloxera is a small, sap sucking insect related to the aphid that feeds on the roots and leaves of the grape vine.

Eventually the vine dies because the nutrients it needs to grow stems, leaves and grapes is cut off by fungal infections and root deformations. There is no treatment for phylloxera other than grubbing the vines out of the ground and burning them.

Vines Saved by New Rootstock

Some American strains of vine are resistant to the pest and this

Sunset over the Pagos

proved a life saver for the Spanish growers. As the fly spread through Europe, moving ever closer to Spain, the Spanish growers had the time to bring in the disease resistant rootstock from America and graft local varieties of grape vine to them. This also allowed them to standardise the grape varieties used in the production of sherry. The 'mother of all vines', Palomino, continued to be grown for dry wines and Pedro Ximénez and Moscatel were grown for the sweeter versions. They are all white grapes. When the Palomino wine is mixed with wine made from the Pedro Ximénez grape that has been left to dry in the sun to concentrate the sugars, the wine is sweeter and is called cream or amoroso (the word amoroso is Italian and means lovely).

WINE FACT

In 2006 DNA research proved that the Mission grape of California and Latin America is the now rare Palomino negro grape grown in Spain. It had been taken to the New World by Jesuit and Franciscan missionaries back in the 16th Century. Bringing in phylloxera resistant stock from America in the 19th Century completed the round trip for these vines.

The Future For Sherry

As we enter the 21st Century, after over 3,000 years of making popular wines and sherry in the Sherry Triangle, what does the market look like? The answer is, in a word, bleak.

In 1975 there were over 30,000 hectares of vines, in 2015 there were just 7,000. As recently as 2002 total world sales of sherry were over 62 million litres, in 2014 they were half that. Much of the decline is due to reduced sales of the sweeter wines. In some areas of the world, notably the USA, dry sherry is showing signs of a resurgence but there is a long way to go.

Some bodegas are diversifying into traditional wines in other areas of Spain. One at least is entering the whisky market in a clever marketing reversal. The González Byass brand Nomad is a premium blended whisky made from 30 different malt and grain whiskies –mainly from Speyside, in the Highlands– these have been aged for between 5 and 8 years. The whiskies age for an average of six years in Scotland –the last three years blended in butts that have been previously soaked in Oloroso to ensure the perfect assembly of flavours. Subsequently, the blend travels to Jerez, where it continues to mature in barrels that have contained old Pedro Ximénez for a minimum of 12 months.

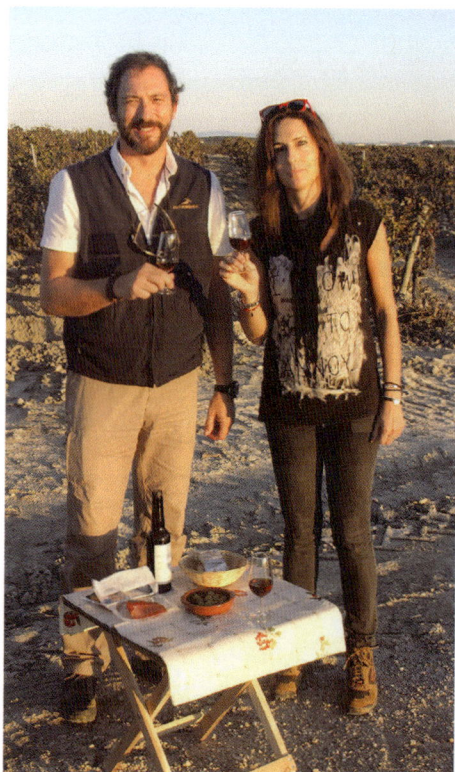

Our Rutasiete guides

Take a Tour

The best way to see the pagos is to take a tour. Rutasiete, based in Jerez de la Frontera, offer a personalised and informed service that encompasses the whole triangle.

Chapter 1 The Story of One Bodega

www.gonzalezbyass.com/en/

www.sherrynotes.com/

Chapter 2 Doña Blanca

Jose Angel Zamora (La epigrafía fenicia del yacimiento del Castillo de Doña Blanca (El Puerto de Santa María, Cádiz) 2004)

J. Lopez Amador (EXCAVACIONES EN DOÑA BLANCA. Se cumplen 35 años. 2014)

Chapter 3 - Jerez de la Frontera

Tourist Information - www.turismojerez.com/index.php/en

The Alcázar - www.jerez.es/index.php?id=471

The Municipal Archaeological Museum - www.jerez.es/webs_municipales/museo

The Royal Andalusian School of Equestrian Art Foundation and the Carriage Museum - www.realescuela.org/en/museoeng.cfm

The Clock Museum - www.spain.info/en/que-quieres/arte/museos/cadiz/museos_de_la_atalaya.html

Moto Cross - www.circuitodejerez.com

Fiestas - www.jerez.es/ciudad/fiestas

Gonzalez Byass Bodegea - www.gonzalezbyass.com

Sandeman - www.sandeman.com/visit-us/jerez

Sherry Tour - www.jerezciudad.com/conoce_jerez/bodegas

Chapter 4 - El Puerto de Santa Maria

Tourist Information - www.turismoelpuerto.com/index.php?setLang=2

Castle of San Marcos - www.cadizturismo.com/turismo-cultural/visitas/cadiz/castillo-de-san-marcos

Ferry to Cádiz Timetable - www.catamaranbahiacadiz.es/horarios.php

Ferias and Fiestas - www.turismoelpuerto.com

Bodega Grant - www.bodegasgrant.com/en

Chapter 5 - Sanlúcar de Barrameda

Tourist Information - www.sanlucar-de-barrameda.com

Castillo de Santiago - www.castillodesantiago.com

Ferry to the Doñana - www.visithuelva.com/activities/activity.asp?Id=224362

Ferias and Fiestas - www.sanlucarturismo.com

Bodega La Cigarrera - www.bodegaslacigarrera.com

Bodegas Hidalgo - La Gitana - www.lagitana.es

Bodegas Barbadillo - www.barbadillo.com/en

Chapter 6 - Inside the Triangle

1904 Map of Pagos in Jerez Municipality - gigapan.com/gigapans/68318

Guided Tours of the Triangle - rutasiete.es

Printed in Great Britain
by Amazon

36375619R00046